paperblanks®
POETRY IN BLOOM

Poetry in Bloom

This cover design, originally crafted by Riviere and Son,
centres around a sensitive plant (*mimosa pudica*) sur-
rounded by chambers containing snowdrops and other
richly hued and contrasting flowers, foliage and butterflies.
The original binding was used for *The Sensitive Plant and
Early Poems* by Percy Bysshe Shelley and is a celebration of
the many moods of the creative spirit.

ISBN: 978-1-4397-5367-5
MINI FORMAT   176 PAGES   LINED
DESIGNED IN CANADA

North America 1-800-277-5887
Europe 800-3333-8005
Japan 0120-177-153

paperblanks.com

paperblanks®
POETRY IN BLOOM

Cette couverture, initialement réalisée par Riviere & Son, se focalise sur la plante sensible (*mimosa pudica*), entourée de chambres dans lesquelles apparaissent des flocons de neige ainsi que des feuillages, fleurs et papillons riches en couleur et en contraste. La reliure originale fut utilisée pour le recueil de Percy Bysshe Shelley, *The Sensitive Plant and Early Poems*, et représente une célébration des différentes humeurs de l'esprit créatif.

Der Einband, dessen Original von den Buchbindern Riviere and Son stammt, zeigt eine schamhafte Sinnpflanze (*mimosa pudica*), umgeben von Schnee-glöckchen und anderen farbenfrohen Blumen, Blättern und Schmetterlingen. Die Originalbindung enthielt das Werk *The Sensitive Plant and Early Poems* des Dichters Percy Bysshe Shelley, und ist eine Hommage an die vielfältigen Stimmen des kreativen Geistes.

Questa copertina, creata in origine da Riviere and Son, rappresenta una pianta sensitiva (*mimosa pudica*) circondata da sezioni decorate con bucaneve e altri fiori, foglie e farfalle dalle tonalità ricche e contrastanti. La rilegatura originale è stata utilizzata per *La pianta sensitiva e primi poemi* di Percy Bysshe Shelley ed è una celebrazione dei numerosi stati d'animo dello spirito creativo.

El motivo central de esta cubierta, que recrea un diseño de Riviere and Son, es una mimosa sensitiva, rodeada de campanillas de invierno y otras flores, plantas y mariposas de tonos vivos. La encuadernación original corresponde a la obra *The Sensitive Plant and Early Poems* de Percy Bysshe Shelley, y celebra las numerosas facetas no solo del espíritu creativo, sino también de la sensi-bilidad poética de principios del siglo XX.

Riviere and Sonによる装丁を再現したデザイン。中央の含羞(はにかみ)草(そう)をぐるりと囲む形で、スノードロップをはじめ、色鮮やかな花々、植物、蝶の図柄が配されています。原版はパーシー・ビッシュ・シェリーの「はにかみ草および初期詩編」で使用されたものであり、豊かな創造性を存分に感じられます。